OSCAR C. DAVIS

A Day in His Life

HEDDRICK MCBRIDE

TABLE OF CONTENTS

CHAPTER 1: A PERFECT START

Oscar C. Davis woke up at precisely 6:17 a.m., the time he had set his alarm for the past three years. The soft buzz of the alarm clock was the first sound of his day, and it was comforting. Consistent. Predictable. He stretched, his limbs brushing the perfectly tucked edges of his blanket. Slowly, he got out of bed and turned to smooth his covers, ensuring there were no wrinkles. Then, he fluffed his pillows and placed them neatly against the headboard.

Oscar's room was his sanctuary. Everything had its place: books lined up by height on the shelf, shoes perfectly lined up beneath his dresser, and a calendar pinned to the wall. Each square of the calendar was filled with neat, color-coded notes—red for school projects, blue for family events, green for personal goals. Today's square read: "Science Fair. Presentation @ 10:30 a.m."

Today was important. He'd spent weeks building his model of a renewable energy-powered city. Every detail was carefully planned: wind turbines that actually spun, solar panels made from reflective foil, and tiny LED lights that illuminated his miniature streets. It was his proudest creation yet.

But first, there were routines to complete. Oscar walked to his door and tapped the frame three times, then headed to the bathroom. He washed his hands, counted to twenty while scrubbing, and dried them on the same towel he'd used the day before. When he returned to his room, he double-checked his backpack: notebooks, pencils, model city instructions. All zipped up and ready. Yet he checked again. And then one more time.

"Oscar! Breakfast!" his mom called from the kitchen.

"Coming!" he replied, glancing at his watch. It was 6:42 a.m. He had just enough time to run through his checklist before heading downstairs.

CHAPTER 2: THE SCIENCE FAIR

By 8:15 a.m., Oscar was in the school's bustling hallway, clutching his model city. His classmates milled around, chatting and laughing. Some gave him curious glances, but he kept his focus on his project, taking careful steps to avoid bumping into anyone.

"Hey, Oscar!" called a familiar voice. It was his best friend, Malik. Malik was everything Oscar wasn't: laid-back, spontaneous, and a little messy. But that was what made their friendship work. Malik didn't mind when Oscar reminded him (repeatedly) to double-check his homework or organize his locker. In return, Malik encouraged Oscar to relax, even if just a little.

"Hey," Oscar said, adjusting the base of his model. "Did you finish your poster?"

"Barely," Malik admitted with a grin. "But it's done. Yours looks awesome, by the way."

"Thanks," Oscar replied, a small smile tugging at his lips. Compliments felt good, but they also made him nervous. What if his project wasn't as good as he thought?

The science fair was held in the gym, where tables were lined up in neat rows. Oscar carefully placed his model on his assigned table and began setting it up. He arranged the pieces meticulously, adjusting the placement of each tiny house and streetlamp until everything felt right.

When the judges arrived, Oscar took a deep breath and launched into his presentation. He explained how his city's wind turbines generated clean energy, how the solar panels powered homes, and how the LED streetlights reduced electricity usage. His words flowed easily; he'd practiced this speech dozens of times in front of his mirror.

The judges nodded, impressed. One of them, a woman with glasses perched on her nose, said, "Your attention to detail is remarkable, Oscar. This is one of the most thoughtful projects we've seen."

Oscar's chest swelled with pride. "Thank you," he said, his voice steady.

SCIENCE

After the science fair, Oscar's teacher, Ms. Carter, stopped him in the hallway. "Oscar, can I talk to you for a moment?" she asked.

"Sure," he said, clutching his backpack straps.

"I noticed how hard you've been working on your project," Ms. Carter said. "But I also see you getting stuck sometimes. Like when you're triple-checking your work or organizing your desk. Those habits can be helpful, but they might also make things harder for you. Have you thought about talking to someone about it?"

Oscar's face grew hot. "I...I don't know," he mumbled. He didn't like talking about his habits. They were just part of who he was.

"There's no pressure," Ms. Carter said gently. "Just know that I'm here if you ever need support."

Oscar nodded, grateful for her understanding. But her words lingered in his mind as he walked home that afternoon. Was there a way to make his habits work for him without feeling trapped by them?

That evening, as he sat at his desk sketching ideas for his next project, his mom came in. "How was the science fair?" she asked.

"Good," Oscar said. "The judges liked my project."

"I'm not surprised," she said with a smile. "You're amazing, Oscar. Just don't be too hard on yourself, okay?"

Oscar nodded, her words echoing Ms. Carter's. Maybe it was time to find a balance. He looked at his model city and smiled. It wasn't perfect, but it was his—a reflection of his hard work, his creativity, and, yes, his OCD. And that was something to be proud of.

After the science fair, Malik introduced Oscar to a new activity: basketball. At first, Oscar was hesitant. The idea of sweating and making mistakes in front of others made him uneasy. But Malik convinced him to come to the community center and try it out.

"Just one game," Malik said. "You'll see. It's fun."

Oscar quickly realized that basketball had its own rhythm. The sound of the ball hitting the court, the swish of the net, the precision of a good pass—it was oddly satisfying. Though he struggled at first, his attention to detail helped him improve. He focused on his shooting form, his footwork, and his timing. Before long, he found himself looking forward to practice.

CHAPTER 5: BUILDING CONNECTIONS

Through basketball, Oscar met new friends, including a girl named Maya who shared his love for science. One day after practice, Maya sat next to Oscar on the bleachers.

"Hey, I heard you're into science stuff," she said, tying her shoelaces.

Oscar nodded. "Yeah, I'm in the robotics club too. What about you?"

"Same," Maya said with a grin. "I'm working on a robot that can sort recyclables. You should come to a meeting sometime."

"Really?" Oscar's eyes lit up. "That sounds awesome. Maybe I will."

"We could use someone like you," Maya said. "Malik keeps saying how detail-oriented you are."

Oscar glanced over at Malik, who gave him a thumbs-up from across the court. "He's exaggerating," Oscar muttered, but he couldn't help but smile.

CHAPTER 6: BALANCING ACT

As Oscar's schedule filled up with basketball, robotics, and schoolwork, he found himself facing new challenges. One evening, he sat at the kitchen table with his homework spread out in front of him.

"How's it going?" his mom asked, placing a glass of milk next to him.

"Okay," Oscar said, rubbing his temples. "I just... feel like I'm running out of time. There's so much to do."

"Maybe you need to prioritize," his mom suggested. "What's most important right now?"

Oscar thought for a moment. "I guess the math homework... but I also want to finish the robotics design. And then there's practice tomorrow."

"Take it one step at a time," his mom said. "You're doing great, Oscar. Just don't forget to breathe."

During a basketball game, Oscar missed a critical shot in the final moments. As the buzzer sounded, signaling their loss, he hung his head.

"It's just one game," Malik said, clapping him on the back.

"Yeah, but it was my fault," Oscar muttered.

Maya joined them, crossing her arms. "You're always so hard on yourself. You think one missed shot defines the whole game? We're a team, Oscar. We win and lose together."

Oscar looked up, meeting her determined gaze. "Thanks, guys."

"Next time, we'll win," Malik said confidently. "As long as you stop overthinking everything."

At the robotics competition, Maya nudged Oscar as they waited for the judges' results. "You nervous?"

"A little," Oscar admitted.

"Don't be. Our robot killed it out there," Maya said.

When the first-place announcement came, their team erupted in cheers. Malik high-fived Oscar, and Maya grinned.

"Told you," she said. "Your design was flawless."

ROBOTICS
CHAMPIONSHIP
ROBOTICS
CHAMPIONSHIP

Oscar C. Davis

Inspired by his experiences, Oscar decided to give a presentation about OCD during a school assembly. As he spoke, he saw nods of understanding in the crowd.

Afterward, a younger student approached him. "Thanks for sharing that. I... I thought I was the only one who felt like this."

Oscar smiled. "You're not alone. Just remember, it's okay to ask for help."

By the end of the year, Oscar had grown in ways he hadn't thought possible. Basketball taught him teamwork, robotics fueled his creativity, and his friendships gave him the support he needed. While his OCD was still a part of his life, it no longer defined him. Instead, it became one of many traits that made him who he was. And for Oscar C. Davis, that was more than enough.

- Be patient and kind. It's okay if your friend has routines that seem unusual.

- Listen when they talk about how they feel. A little understanding goes a long way.

- Celebrate their strengths, like attention to detail or creativity.

- Include them in activities but understand if they need a moment to adjust.

- Be supportive and understanding. Create a safe space for your child to express themselves.

- Help them develop coping strategies, like breaking tasks into smaller steps.

- Work with teachers or counselors to address challenges at school.

- Encourage their strengths and remind them they're more than their OCD.

○ Foster an inclusive classroom environment. Flexibility with routines can help students with OCD.

○ Collaborate with parents and counselors to understand the student's needs.

○ Recognize and encourage the student's strengths, like problem-solving or precision.

○ Provide gentle guidance if they get stuck on a task, and celebrate their efforts.

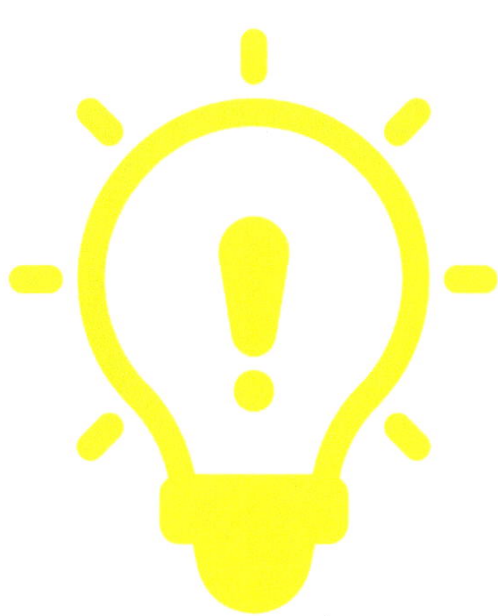

VISIT

www.mcbridestories.com

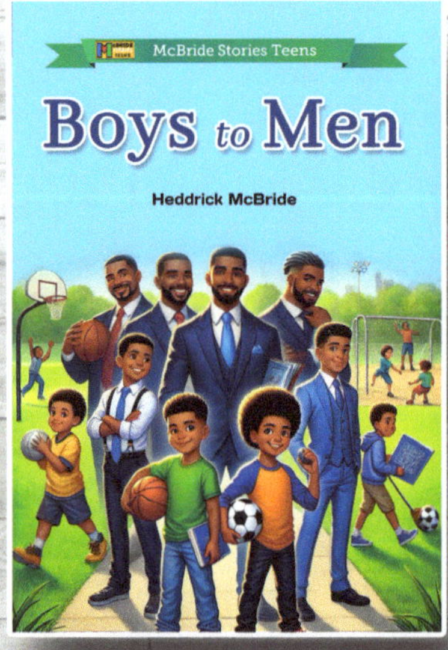

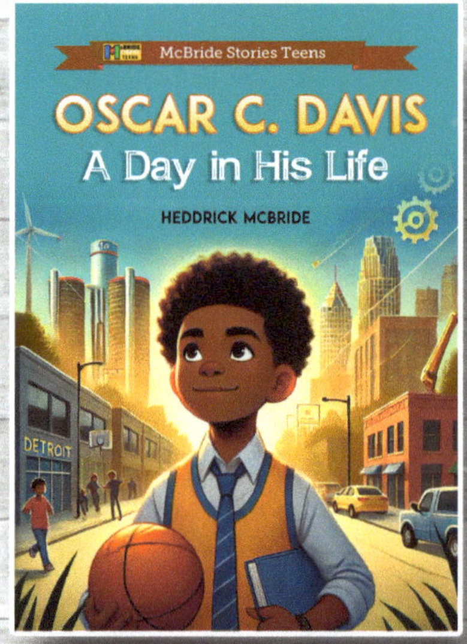

VISIT
www.mcbridestories.com

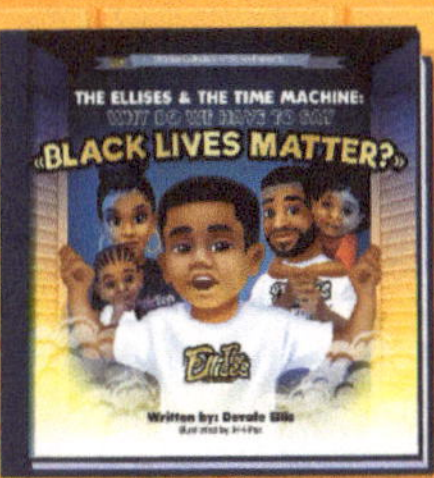

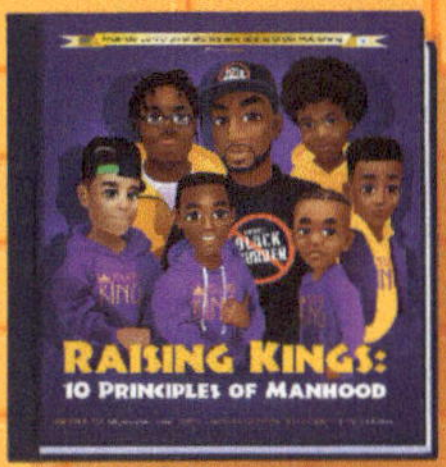
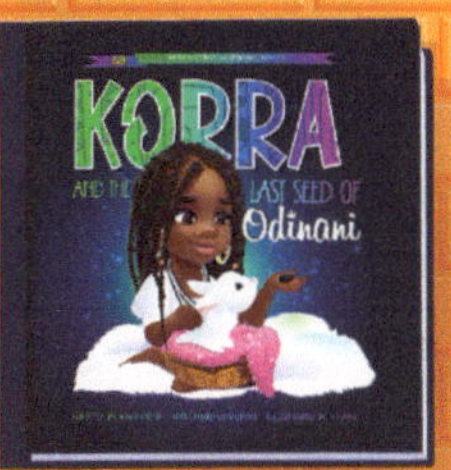